COMPOSER'S CHOICE

CAROLYN MILLER

ABOUT THE SERIES

The Composer's Choice series showcases piano works by an exclusive group of composers. Each collection contains classic piano pieces that were carefully chosen by the composer, as well as brand-new pieces written especially for the series. Helpful performance notes are also included.

ISBN 978-1-4803-6659-6

WILLIS MUSIC

EXCLUSIVELY DISTRIBUTED BY

HAL•LEONARD®
CORPORATION

7777 W. BLUEMOUND RD. P.O. BOX 13819 MILWAUKEE, WI 53213

Visit Hal Leonard Online at
www.halleonard.com

FROM THE COMPOSER

You will find some of my favorite solos in this collection. There are a variety of styles, but all are fun to play and have technical value for the student. I hope piano students of all ages will enjoy playing and performing these pieces.

Enjoy!

Carolyn Miller

CONTENTS

ALLISON'S SONG

This solo needs to be played very *legato*. Play musically and soften the ends of phrases. The left hand (LH) should be relaxed throughout, and when the second finger crosses over on beats 2 and 4, the wrist should have an upward release. Be sure to keep a relaxed right hand (RH) wrist while playing the intervals of sixths in measures 9-17. Let the music flow.

LITTLE WALTZ IN E MINOR

Feel the movement of this delicate waltz. In the middle section, I have a vision of Cinderella and her Prince Charming dancing happily in a large ballroom. The LH could be practiced as blocked chords throughout, and the RH should float above the accompaniment. Let the dancing begin!

REFLECTIONS

This is one of my favorite solos. I love the chord changes in the LH at the beginning; practice them as blocked chords. The RH must have a deep singing tone with a softer eighth-note accompaniment in the bass. Play the theme with lots of feeling; avoid sounding "mechanical." *Crescendo* into a phrase and *decrescendo* at the end of a phrase. For instance, the last RH note in measures 4 and 12 should be softer. Make it a musical presentation and enjoy!

RIPPLES IN THE WATER

This solo was originally in a book titled *Chords Rule*. When I composed it, I wanted to especially emphasize chord inversions. As you can see, the LH is almost ALL inversions. They should be played gently, and not like an exercise. Learning the inversions in G, F, D, A and E-flat will make this much easier to play.

I added a few notes to this updated version. There is a slight variation in the RH in measures 4, 8, 10, 12, 14-16. The Coda has also been slightly extended. Make the piece flow like ripples in the water!

ARPEGGIO WALTZ

Students are sometimes "forced" to learn arpeggios; with this piece they can now reap the benefits of their hard work! "Arpeggio Waltz" comes from a book titled *Arpeggios Rule* and is filled with (you guessed it!) arpeggios. This new version is a variation of the original. The beginning theme has been changed to 1,2,3,1,3,5 instead of 1,3,5,1,3,5. In measures 19 and 27 the RH has an extended melody. Also, the chord in measure 23 has been altered, and variations in measure 29-32 have been added.

Students should play with a relaxed hand position while feeling a gentle waltz rhythm. A slight raising of the wrist on the staccato notes will make them sound gentler. Let the melody soar as your arms float over the keys.

TRUMPET IN THE NIGHT

Learning the LH correctly is essential in this piece, so that it can move easily while your RH brings out the melody. *Crescendo* and *decrescendo* appropriately as the melody rises and falls. Learning the blues scale in F will help you at measures 19-20. Note the return to even eighth notes at the end, but most importantly, enjoy playing the blues! P.S. Feel free to improvise.

TOCCATA SEMPLICE

Here's an exciting new piece! The rhythmic pattern in measure 1 needs to be clean and crisp every time it is played. Pedaling is important, along with crisp staccato. The chord structure is the same for measure 1-4 and 41-44. Look also for the hidden melody at the bottom notes of the RH triads in measures 41-46. Accents are very important in this solo: play with firm fingers and lots of energy.

RHAPSODY IN A MINOR

This new solo has many different moods. Perhaps start with mastering the ending before anything else: practice the RH in blocked A Minor inversions. The opening is rather melancholic-sounding, yet lyrical. The LH supports the hopeful melody with rolling arpeggios. This is followed by a more dance-like section. Play deep into the keys, especially in the closing section, and aim for a flamboyant finale.

Allison's Song

Carolyn Miller

Little Waltz in E Minor

Carolyn Miller

Reflections

Carolyn Miller

Ripples in the Water

Carolyn Miller

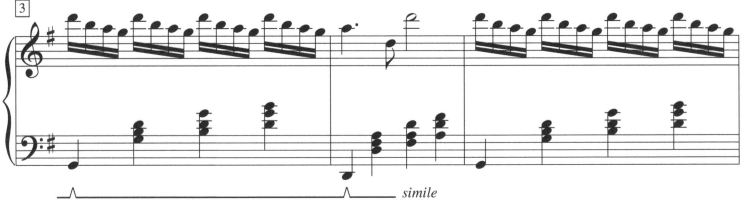

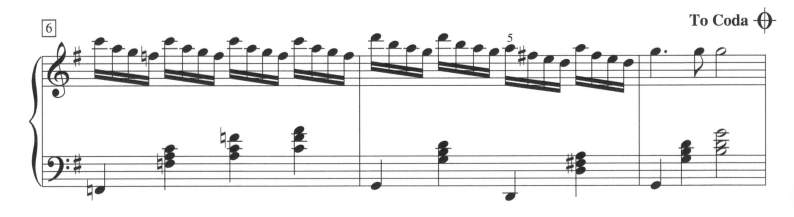

D.C. al Coda

Arpeggio Waltz

Carolyn Miller

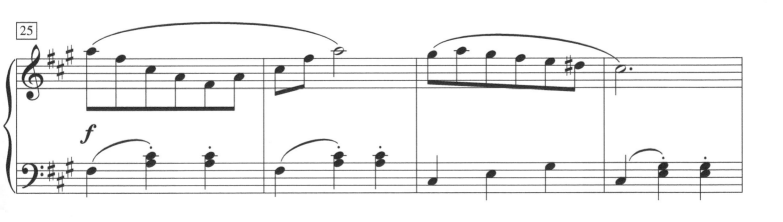

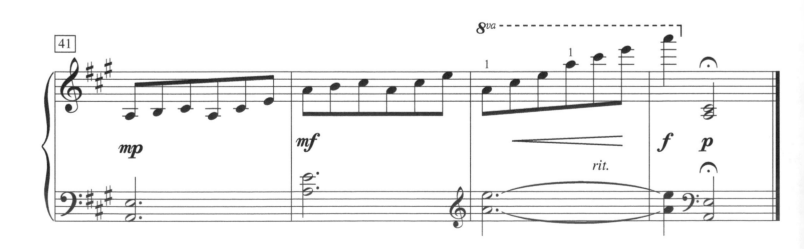

For Marie Speziale

Trumpet in the Night

Carolyn Miller

Toccata Semplice

Carolyn Miller

Rhapsody in A Minor

Carolyn Miller

A DOZEN A DAY SONGBOOK SERIES

BROADWAY, MOVIE AND POP HITS

Arranged by Carolyn Miller

The *A Dozen a Day Songbook* series contains wonderful Broadway, movie and pop hits that may be used as companion pieces to the memorable technique exercises in the *A Dozen a Day* series. They are also suitable as supplements for ANY method!

Mini
Early Elementary

A DOZEN A DAY SONGBOOK

Broadway, Movie and Pop Hits

Any Dream Will Do • Can You Feel the Love Tonight • A Dream Is a Wish Your Heart Makes
Heigh-Ho • I'm Popeye the Sailor Man • It's a Grand Night for Singing • Lean on Me
Love Me Tender • So Long, Farewell • You'll Never Walk Alone

THE WILLIS MUSIC COMPANY

MINI
EARLY ELEMENTARY
Songs in the Mini Book:
Any Dream Will Do • Can You Feel the Love Tonight • A Dream Is a Wish Your Heart Makes • Heigh-Ho • I'm Popeye the Sailor Man • It's a Grand Night for Singing • Lean on Me • Love Me Tender • So Long, Farewell • You'll Never Walk Alone.

00416858 Book Only $9.99
00416861 Book/Audio $12.99

PREPARATORY
MID-ELEMENTARY
Songs in the Preparatory Book:
The Bare Necessities • Do-Re-Mi • Getting to Know You • Heart and Soul • Little April Shower • Part of Your World • The Surrey with the Fringe on Top • Swinging on a Star • The Way You Look Tonight • Yellow Submarine.

00416859 Book Only $9.99
00416862 Book/Audio $12.99

BOOK 1
LATER ELEMENTARY
Songs in Book 1:
Cabaret • Climb Ev'ry Mountain • Give a Little Whistle • If I Were a Rich Man • Let It Be • Rock Around the Clock • Twist and Shout • The Wonderful Thing About Tiggers • Yo Ho (A Pirate's Life for Me) • Zip-A-Dee-Doo-Dah.

00416860 Book Only $9.99
00416863 Book/Audio $12.99

BOOK 2
EARLY INTERMEDIATE
Songs in Book 2:
Hallelujah • I Dreamed A Dream • I Walk the Line • I Want to Hold Your Hand • In the Mood • Moon River • Once Upon A Dream • This Land is Your Land • A Whole New World • You Raise Me Up.

00119241 Book Only $9.99
00119242 Book/Audio $14.99

Prices, content, and availability subject to change without notice.

WILLIS MUSIC

EXCLUSIVELY DISTRIBUTED BY
HAL•LEONARD®

www.willispianomusic.com   **www.facebook.com/willispianomusic**

CLASSIC PIANO REPERTOIRE

The *Classic Piano Repertoire* series includes popular as well as lesser-known pieces from a select group of composers out of the Willis piano archives. Every piece has been newly engraved and edited with the aim to preserve each composer's original intent and musical purpose.

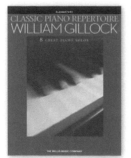

WILLIAM GILLOCK - ELEMENTARY

8 Great Piano Solos

Dance in Ancient Style • Little Flower Girl of Paris • On a Paris Boulevard • Rocking Chair Blues • Sliding in the Snow • Spooky Footsteps • A Stately Sarabande • Stormy Weather.

00416957 ....$8.99

EDNA MAE BURNAM - ELEMENTARY

8 Great Piano Solos

The Clock That Stopped • The Friendly Spider • A Haunted House • New Shoes • The Ride of Paul Revere • The Singing Cello • The Singing Mermaid • Two Birds in a Tree.

00110228 ....$8.99

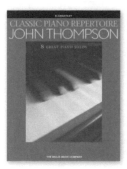

JOHN THOMPSON - ELEMENTARY

9 Great Piano Solos

Captain Kidd • Drowsy Moon • Dutch Dance • Forest Dawn • Humoresque • Southern Shuffle • Tiptoe • Toy Ships • Up in the Air.

00111968 ....$8.99

LYNN FREEMAN OLSON - EARLY TO LATER ELEMENTARY

14 Great Piano Solos

Caravan • Carillon • Come Out! Come Out! (Wherever You Are) • Halloween Dance • Johnny, Get Your Hair Cut! • Jumping the Hurdles • Monkey on a Stick • Peter the Pumpkin Eater • Pony Running Free • Silent Shadows • The Sunshine Song • Tall Pagoda • Tubas and Trumpets • Winter's Chocolatier.

00294722 ....$9.99

WILLIAM GILLOCK - INTERMEDIATE TO ADVANCED

12 Exquisite Piano Solos

Classic Carnival • Etude in A Major (The Coral Sea) • Etude in E Minor • Etude in G Major (Toboggan Ride) • Festive Piece • A Memory of Vienna • Nocturne • Polynesian Nocturne • Sonatina in Classic Style • Sonatine • Sunset • Valse Etude.

00416912 ....$12.99

EDNA MAE BURNAM - INTERMEDIATE TO ADVANCED

13 Memorable Piano Solos

Butterfly Time • Echoes of Gypsies • Hawaiian Leis • Jubilee! • Longing for Scotland • Lovely Senorita • The Mighty Amazon River • Rumbling Rumba • The Singing Fountain • Song of the Prairie • Storm in the Night • Tempo Tarantelle • The White Cliffs of Dover.

00110229 ....$12.99

JOHN THOMPSON - INTERMEDIATE TO ADVANCED

12 Masterful Piano Solos

Andantino (from Concerto in D Minor) • The Coquette • The Faun • The Juggler • Lagoon • Lofty Peaks • Nocturne • Rhapsody Hongroise • Scherzando in G Major • Tango Carioca • Valse Burlesque • Valse Chromatique.

00111969 ....$12.99

LYNN FREEMAN OLSON - EARLY TO MID-INTERMEDIATE

13 Distinctive Piano Solos

Band Wagon • Brazilian Holiday • Cloud Paintings • Fanfare • The Flying Ship • Heroic Event • In 1492 • Italian Street Singer • Mexican Serenade • Pageant Dance • Rather Blue • Theme and Variations • Whirlwind.

00294720 ....$9.99

WILLIS MUSIC

www.willispianomusic.com

www.facebook.com/willispianomusic

EXCLUSIVELY DISTRIBUTED BY

HAL•LEONARD®

Prices, content, and availability subject to change without notice.